Embassy was substantially rebuilt after war service as a minesweeper, before resuming south coast excursion duties. She is seen here at Bournemouth Pier in 1964.

COVER: *Waverley has become well known as 'The Last Seagoing Paddle Steamer In The World' since being acquired for preservation in 1973. She was built as late as 1947 by A & J Inglis for the London & North Eastern Railway.*

PADDLE STEAMERS

John Woodhams

Oakfield Publications

CONTENTS

ACKNOWLEDGEMENTS

I would like to thank all those friends and fellow enthusiasts who have so kindly allowed me to use their photographs in this book, which are acknowledged as follows:

Colin Caddy, Page 5 (lower), 6 (upper), 7 (both), 8 (both), 10 (both), 13 (lower), 22 (lower).
John H. Meredith, Page 1, 4 (upper), 9, 12 (both), 13 (upper), 14 (upper), 17 (both), 18 (upper), 20.
Alan Kittridge, Page 2.
H. Cameron-White, Page 16.
Nick James, Page 11.
Hjejlen ApS (Ric Kristensen), Page 22 (upper), 29 (upper).
A. Scrimali, Page 29 (lower).
Ernst Schmidt, Page 30 (upper).
Kpt Karlheinz Eder, Page 30 (lower).
Museum der Deutschen Binnenschiffahrt, Page 18 (lower).
Weisse Flotte Dresden, Page 26 (lower), 27 (upper).
KD, Page 25.
DDSG, Page 26 (upper).
Showboat Avoca, Page 27 (lower).
Tourism South Australia, Page 28 (upper).
AS Oplandske Dampskibsselskab, Page 28 (lower).
Author/Author's collection, Cover, Page 3, 4 (lower), 5 (upper and middle), 6 (lower), 14 (lower), 15, 21 (both), 23, 24.

British Library Cataloguing in Publication Data
Woodhams John
Paddle Steamers
1. Paddle Steamers
1. Title
623. 82432
ISBN 0-9516946-0-X

Printed by
Isle of Wight County Press,
29 High Street, Newport, Isle of Wight.
PO30 1ST

Compton Castle, one of the delightful River Dart steamers, heads off on a river cruise. The hull still survives, although rebuilt, and the engines are separately preserved on the Isle of Wight.

Henry Bell's Comet of 1812. This pioneer craft featured two paddle wheels each side of the hull. The original engine is now preserved in the Science Museum, London, and a replica of the complete vessel was built in Scotland in the 1960s.

PIONEERS TO OCEAN CROSSINGS

The first successful steamship with paddle wheel propulsion was the *Charlotte Dundas* of 1801, designed by William Symington and sponsored by Lord Dundas. The single paddle wheel was located at the stern of the vessel which it was hoped would be used as a tug on the Forth and Clyde Canal. The first attempt was not successful, and a second vessel with the same name followed a year later.

There are various references to paddle propulsion dating back to Roman times, when oxen were used as a power source. The Chinese used man powered paddle wheels — an idea later pursued by Leonardo da Vinci.

In the early 18th century Denis Papin, a Frenchman, proposed a steam powered vessel, and is thought to have constructed a paddle boat. Several early attempts to apply steam power to boats emanated from France, notably the *Pyroscaphe* of the Marquis de Jouffroy d'Abbans of 1783.

In America, John Fitch designed and built a ship which was propelled by a linked system of oars powered by steam. A fellow countryman, Richard Fulton, developed the *Clermont* from his earlier observation of the *Charlotte Dundas* in Scotland. The 133 feet long *Clermont* initiated a service between New York and Albany on the Hudson River, although she was later renamed *North River*.

It was five years later in 1812 that Britain's first commercial steamer service commenced between Glasgow and Greenock, operated by the *Comet* designed by Henry Bell. The ship ran successfully for eight years before running aground and becoming a total wreck.

In 1815 a service between London and Gravesend was started by the Clyde built paddler *Margery*. This 73 ft. long vessel became the first steamer to cross the channel to Le Havre after her sale to a French operator. However, a further seven years elapsed before the first commercial crossing of the channel by a steamship.

Gradually the steamship established itself, and ship owners started to look towards the possibility of ocean crossings.

Gordon was one of a quartet of very distinctive coke fired paddlers built to maintain the Woolwich Free Ferry across the Thames.

Although weather conditions were still a most important consideration, ships were no longer entirely dependent on the wind and it became feasible to programme a ship's operations more accurately. However, the price of this convenience meant that large parts of the ship were taken up with engines, boilers and bunkers.

The American built *Savannah* is generally regarded as the first steamship to cross the Atlantic in 1819, although she was a converted schooner and steam driven collapsible paddle wheels were only used for part of the journey. The crossing was made because her owners hoped to sell the ship in Britain, although she later returned to America.

The first British steamer to make the crossing was the PS *Rising Star* in 1821. This unusual warship had three keels, with the two paddle wheels placed in between them. Another unusual design was *London Engineer* which had two internal paddle wheels in an airtight compartment. Compressed air was used to lower the water level so that only the lower blades of the paddles were submerged. Also in 1821, the first iron hulled steamship appeared, PS *Aaron*

Lincoln Castle was one of three ferries with car deck used for the Hull to New Holland service across the Humber estuary. She was withdrawn in 1978 with boiler problems, and the service was discontinued completely shortly afterwards, with the opening of the new suspension bridge.

Largest of the Southern Railway's Portsmouth fleet was Whippingham, built by the Fairfield Company in 1930. She is pictured at Ryde on her last day in service in 1962.

The Ryde was the last paddle steamer to be built for the Southern Railway, being delivered in 1937. Slightly smaller than the Whippingham at 566 tons, she remained in service until 1969, before being sold for use as a nightclub.

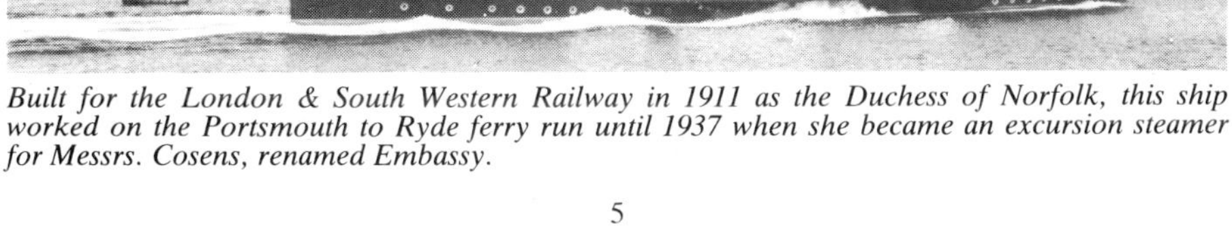

Built for the London & South Western Railway in 1911 as the Duchess of Norfolk, this ship worked on the Portsmouth to Ryde ferry run until 1937 when she became an excursion steamer for Messrs. Cosens, renamed Embassy.

Built for the Southampton to Cowes ferry service in 1927, a small number of cars could be carried on the deck of Princess Elizabeth. Following an uncertain period after final withdrawal she became a floating restaurant, first in London, and subsequently in Paris.

Manby was built in sections at Tipton, Staffordshire, and taken in sections to London for assembly, eventually crossing the channel to enter service on the Seine.

The year 1836 saw the inauguration of regular transatlantic crossings by paddle steamers. The first ship to cross entirely by steam power was in fact the PS *Sirius*, a cross channel steamer totally unsuited to such an ocean passage. Only hours after her arrival in New York, Brunel's *Great Western* appeared, and thus the challenge for record crossings (The Blue Riband) was begun.

Later that same year Samuel Cunard successfully negotiated a contract with the British authorities to carry transatlantic mail, from which grew the mighty Cunard company. Four ships were built by Robert Napier, who became one of Cunard's partners, for the service, which was inaugurated by PS *Britannia* on 4th July, 1840 from Liverpool to Halifax, Nova Scotia. Each of the four ships was 207 feet long and carried 115 passengers in addition to cargo. In 1856 the first iron Cunard ship appeared, the *Persia*, and she held the Blue Riband for the next six years when the *Scotia*, Cunard's last paddler, entered service.

In 1849 the Collins Line tried to break Cunard's virtual monopoly with four paddle steamers, but a string of unfortunate accidents caused the failure of the company within a decade.

Lorna Doone started life as HMS Atherstone, one of a batch of minesweepers built for the Royal Navy in 1916, and with very similar lines to traditional excursion steamers. She joined the Red Funnel fleet at Southampton in 1949, after several seasons cruising in the Thames estuary.

When built in 1888, Monarch was the largest excursion vessel on the south coast, and was finally scrapped in 1950 after a working life which included naval service in both world wars.

Isambard Kingdom Brunel, engineer of the Great Western Railway, had long had an interest in steamships and persuaded his directors to form the Great Western Steamship Company to operate a service to New York, for which he designed the *Great Western*. The ship was launched in 1837, and, as already mentioned, first crossed the Atlantic to arrive only one day after the much smaller *Sirius*. With a length of 236 feet the ship had two engines which would drive each paddle independently or coupled together. The *Great Western* was followed by the *Great Britain*, a screw steamer (although originally intended as a paddler), but Brunel's greatest ship, the *Great Eastern*, was a composite of the two methods, designed to operate to the Far East without stopping for bunkers.

Commissioned by the Eastern Steam Navigation Company in 1852, the ship was at 692 feet the largest merchant ship to date. The paddle wheels were 60 feet in diameter and designed to have about half the power of the screw. She was launched on the Thames in 1858 after many problems, but her owners were by this time in financial difficulties them-

Iron hulled Premier was built by Wm Denny in 1846 and ended her working life with Cosens operating from Weymouth 92 years later.

selves, and soon went into liquidation. The massive five funnelled ship set out on trials with Brunel on board, but he suffered a stroke and died a year later. The vessel never lived up to its expectations and was placed on the Atlantic run until becoming a cable layer in 1865, and eventually being broken up in 1888.

The classic view of an excursion steamer at Lulworth Cove, where passengers were normally landed over the bow of the ship.

Empress and Victoria were the last two British excursion steamers with oscillating engines. Empress was built at Poplar in 1879, whilst Victoria was actually built at Rotterdam five years later.

Emperor of India is pictured at winter lay-up at Weymouth. She was built by Thornycroft at Southampton in 1906, but her appearance was altered after World War II by the fitting of a new funnel and additional superstructure.

FERRIES AND EXCURSION STEAMERS

The first regular cross channel ferry service from Dover to Calais commenced in 1821 using the 90 ton paddle steamer *Rob Roy*, but already regular sailings were being undertaken to Ireland and the Isle of Man from the British mainland.

In 1824 the General Steam Navigation Company was formed, which offered a service from London to Boulogne, Calais and Ostend. Other services linked the Thames towns with Kent coast ports, and even London with Edinburgh. The Isle of Man Steam Packet Company began operations in 1830 with PS *Mona's Isle*.

However, many ferry services were of a much less ambitious nature. On the Thames from 1840, the Watermen's Steam Packet Company offered services in competition with the Woolwich company which ran as far up river as Richmond. Many other concerns tried to gain a share of the traffic with varying degrees of success, and eventually, in 1904, the London County Council sought an Act of Parliament to enable it to run its own ships. For this operation 30 paddle steamers were built, but within three years all services were withdrawn. The ships were sold far and wide, but one of them, *Gresham*, found its way to Poland where it still exists.

The well known Woolwich Free Ferry was started by the LCC in 1890. The three ships used originally on the cross river service were replaced by four paddle steamers which maintained the link until withdrawal in 1969, when replaced by diesels.

Regular paddle steamer services to the Isle of Wight commenced in the mid 19th century. The three paddlers of the Port of Portsmouth and Ryde Steam Packet Company were later joined by the Southsea and Isle of Wight Steam Ferry Company, amalgamating in 1876 to form the Port of Portsmouth and Ryde United Steam Packet Company. This concern was taken over just four years later jointly by the London and South Western and London Brighton & South Coast Railways, which both ran into Portsmouth.

For a short time the PS *Carrier* maintained a train ferry service between Hayling Island and Bembridge Harbour. The deck of this unusual vessel was fitted with twin railway lines and was built at Greenock in 1858 for the River Tay services operated by the Edinburgh, Perth and Dundee Railway Company. The short lived Isle of Wight service was started by the IW Marine Transit Company in 1884, but eight years later the vessel went to Scandinavian owners. The first train ferry service ran on the River Forth from Granton to Burntisland, also operated by the Edinburgh, Perth and Dundee concern.

Originally named Duke of Devonshire, and built for the Devon Dock, Pier & Steamship Co. in 1896, Consul later passed to P&A Campbell, and then Cosens, who operated her from Weymouth. She was scrapped at Southampton in 1968.

The Portsmouth to Ryde service passed into Southern Railway hands and eventually became part of British Railways in 1948. The Southern Railway ordered no less than seven new paddle steamers between 1924 and 1937. The last built, PS *Ryde,* was withdrawn at the end of the 1969 season.

The other railway owned service to the Island operated between Lymington and Yarmouth. In 1884 the LSWR took over the Solent Steamship Company which had commenced with one small, but appropriately named ship, the *Solent,* in 1850. The last conventional paddler on this route was PS *Freshwater,* built locally at Cowes in 1927, and sold for excursion work in 1959, but *Farringford* was a diesel electric double ended paddle car ferry used on the route.

The double ended vehicle ferry is not unusual, but in the 1880s three double

Although built in the late 1940s for P&A Campbell, Bristol Queen and her sister Cardiff Queen had fairly short working lives. Surprisingly they retained open bridges to the end.

ended passenger steamers were built for the Portsmouth and Ryde service. It was intended that such a design would reduce turn round time. The *Greenore* on Carlingford Lough followed the same principle, as did the *Countess of Kellie* used by the Caledonian Railway at Alloa.

The Southampton to Cowes service has been maintained by Red Funnel — trading name of the Southampton, Isle of Wight and South of England Royal Mail Steam Packet Company. Although it had ordered new motor ships in the early 1930s, its last paddle steamer was not delivered until 1936. Built locally by Thornycroft, the 393 tons *Gracie Fields* was lost returning from Dunkirk in 1940. The *Lord Elgin* was built in 1876 and passed to Red Funnel in 1909. She was not withdrawn until 1955, but at the end of a long career was relegated to cargo duties. Ferry services across the Humber estuary were maintained until 1978 by paddle steamers when the *Lincoln Castle* was withdrawn with boiler problems. *Lincoln Castle* was built in 1940, the last of a trio of broadly similar ships with the after deck open for transport of vehicles. Sister ships *Tattershall Castle* and

A mere 20 years old, Bristol Queen faces an uncertain future in a Bristol dry dock. Rising costs, declining excursion traffic, and damage to a paddle wheel led to the demise of Campbell's last paddle steamers.

In June 1950 PS Glen Gower, another Campbell ship, was photographed approaching Brighton's Palace Pier.

Kingswear Castle was built in 1924 for the River Dart Steamboat Co., although her engines are 20 years older, being taken from a previous vessel of the same name. She has been restored by the Paddle Steamer Preservation Society, and in 1985 recommenced regular sailings on the Rivers Thames and Medway.

Formerly the Jeanie Deans, and sister ship to Waverley, the Queen of the South made a brave attempt to revive Thames cruises in the 1960s. However, the venture met with only limited success, and the ship was sold to Belgian shipbreakers.

Wingfield Castle were built in 1934 at West Hartlepool. The diesel *Farringford* was later used on the route, which ceased operation on completion of the new Humber road bridge.

A network of ferry services has operated on the Mersey, the first steamship, *Princess Charlotte,* being introduced on a service between Eastham and Liverpool in 1826. The Wallasey and Birkenhead ferry services were taken over by the local authorities, and by the turn of the century the days of the paddle steamer were numbered, Birkenhead having ordered its last paddler in 1894. In America, paddle steamer ferries were used in San Francisco Bay, but the opening of the Golden Gate Bridge in 1937 prompted a decline in traffic, and the last paddler was withdrawn in 1957, when the *Eureka* suffered a mechanical failure. American paddle steamers played an important role in developing river traffic before the advent of railways, and the mighty stern wheelers of the Mississippi are undoubtedly the best well known. In 1870 two stern wheelers the *Robert E. Lee* and the *Natchez* raced for three days from New Orleans to St. Louis.

On the Hudson River, Fulton had commenced a service with his *Clermont* in 1816, and other services from New York to Long Island, for example.

Paddle steamers played similar roles in opening up large inland areas of the Murray River in Australia, and paddle

Waverley seen here in pre-preservation days, sporting buff funnels. Note the various detail differences with Queen of the South.

Medway Queen spent most of her working life from 1924 to 1963 as an excursion steamer in the Thames and Medway areas, although during the war she was used in the Dunkirk evacuation, and, in fact, rescued some 7,000 troops, in no less then seven trips.

ferries may still be found on India's great waterway the Ganges. Three stern wheelers, *Hebe*, *Palta* and *Bhadra* survive at Patna.

The largest paddle steamer ferry ever built was the *Greater Detroit* of 7,739 tons, built in 1923. Operated by the Detroit & Cleveland Navigation Company on Great Lakes passenger services she was 520 feet long, 58 feet beam and 15 feet 6 inches draught, and she could maintain a speed of 19 knots. With a fairly high superstructure, stability was maintained by large trimming tanks in the sponsons. Typical of other Great Lakes steamers was the *Kingston*, a mere 288 feet long and 2,925 tons. She was built in 1901 at Toronto, for Canada Steamship Lines.

A trip on a steamboat in the early 19th century was a great novelty, and a new experience, and the pioneer ferry

After withdrawal Medway Queen became a floating restaurant/nightclub on the Isle of Wight's River Medina. By 1984 she was in a very derelict condition, but was refloated and returned to the Medway for eventual restoration. This view shows her being made ready for positioning on the pontoon for the journey back from the south coast.

operators soon realised that additional passengers could be attracted to their vessels purely for pleasure. With the growth of the railway systems and the development of seaside holiday patterns the pure excursion paddle steamer was born. Sometimes fierce competition gave rise to some rather optimistic claims regarding the speed and comfort of the ships employed! However the size, splendour and speed of the excursion steamers improved and day trips to France from south coast ports were common by the 1930s.

Londoners enjoyed Thames cruises to Southend and Clacton, the most well known ships being operated by the General Steam Navigation Company. Their last paddle steamer, the *Crested Eagle*, was built in 1925 at Cowes, and was equipped for oil fuel. Other ships in the fleet were *Golden Eagle* and *Royal Eagle*.

Glaswegians were also able to enjoy cruises on the Firth of Clyde. Excessive drinking on many cruises prompted the Clyde Steam Packet Company to build the *Ivanhoe* in 1880, and to operate it as a dry ship on runs to the Isle of Arran!

The name of P&A Campbell is immediately associated with excursion ships of the Bristol Channel. However, the Campbell operation started on the Clyde, and it was brothers Peter and Alan, sons of the founder, who moved to the Bristol Channel when competition from the railway companies became too intense. Campbell's English operations began with the *Waverley*, but another ex-Clyde steamer, the *Bonnie Doon*, had begun cruising from Bristol to Ilfracombe in 1886. Thirteen years later this ship joined the Campbell fleet. Apart from the popular Bristol to Ilfracombe cruises, a network of excursions grew to include South Wales ports, and destinations such as Lundy Island. After the second world war Campbell's ordered two new ships, *Bristol Queen* and *Cardiff Queen* which were regarded by many as the finest paddlers anywhere in Britain, but their working lives lasted a mere 20 years.

Paddle steamer excursions on the River Dart commenced in 1859 with the *Pilot* and the River Dart Steamboat Company continued in operation until the 1960s. Two of its former ships survive, *Kingswear Castle* is still sailing whilst *Compton Castle*, after abortive attempts to use her as a cafe/restaurant, became a flower shop and coffee lounge in 1990 at Lemon Quay, Truro. In the intervening years when the future looked uncertain the engines were sold to the owners of the Blackgang Chine Theme Park on the Isle of Wight, where they now form the centrepiece of a maritime museum.

An advertisement for east coast excursions dating from the early 1900s.

Last paddle tug on the Clyde was Flying Scotsman built in 1898 for the Clyde Shipping Co. by J. P. Renoldson & Sons, South Shields.

PADDLE TUGS

Large ocean going sailing ships were difficult vessels to manoeuvre in and out of port, and small steam tugs soon developed an important role in assisting larger ships to and from their berths. Early steamships were rather underpowered, and sometimes their towing ability was of doubtful value, but gradually performance improved.

The steam tug first appeared on the Clyde in 1819, seven years after Henry Bell's *Comet,* although *Charlotte Dundas* had been used to tow other vessels during trials in 1801.

Thames based tugs would usually tow outward bound ships as far as the river estuary, and gradually the practice of looking for an inbound ship developed. This practice became known as seeking, and was pioneered by Richard Ross of Gravesend. As tugs became more powerful and their range increased (early tugs often carried insufficient bunkers to successfully complete their tasks) they would look for homeward bound ships farther out to sea, and Thames tugs would often venture as far as the Isle of Wight. As more operators started seeking, competition for work grew, and sometimes a tug would disappear at night without even navigation lights to rendevous with a ship! Even more hazardous perhaps, was to reverse the navigation lights in order to confuse rival tug masters.

Paddle tugs remained popular with ships masters for a long time because the propellers of early screw driven tugs could often be lifted out of the water during a tow.

It was normal practice for steam tug paddles to be driven independently, unlike conventional paddle steamers, where both paddles were driven by a single crankshaft. This allowed superior manoeuvrability, as one wheel could be reversed whilst the other was still set at full ahead. One rather crude alternative tried on the paddle tug *Monarch* of 1833, was a trolley full of chains which could be wheeled from one side of the ship to the other in an attempt to set one paddle wheel lower in the water than the other!

By the time of the first world war, screw tugs had virtually ousted the paddlers, but the Royal Navy continued to use them both in British dockyards and in other ports around the world. Its last steam tugs survived into the 1960s, but in the 1950s a class of seven diesel electric paddle tugs were commissioned.

Several steam paddle tugs survived into the 1960s in north-east England. The 160 ton *Eppleton Hall* finished her

Seen awaiting her next turn of duty at South Shields in 1954 is the paddle tug Reliant, now preserved in the National Maritime Museum, Greenwich.

working life at Seaham Harbour, and in 1967 was sold for scrap. However, she was purchased by an American owner, and on 18th September, 1969 sailed for a new home at the San Francisco Maritime Museum under her own power. Two paddle tugs have been preserved in the UK, the *Reliant* at the National Maritime Museum, Greenwich, and the *John H. Amos*, currently awaiting restoration at Chatham Dockyard.

Paddle tugs were sometimes converted for use as trawlers, which would often entail comparatively longer sea voyages. A purpose-built trawler was commissioned by F. Rushworth of Grimsby in 1870, but during a slump in trade in 1877, a paddle tug owner, William Purdy, of North Shields, decided to use his tug for fishing. The last paddle trawler in the area was the *Hartland*, based at Scarborough.

When withdrawn from service at Seaham Harbour in 1967, the diminutive Eppleton Hall was initially sold for scrap. However, she was rescued and sailed to a new home at the San Francisco Maritime Museum — under her own power!

Heading purposefully through Portsmouth Harbour is the former Admiralty paddle tug Camel. Note the hulk of the sailing ship Foudroyant in the background.

In mainland Europe large river paddle tugs were built for both the Danube and the Rhine. These were often sleek and elegant twin funnelled vessels looking more like excursion steamers than the squat, harbour tugs. Several German owned Rhine tugs were scuttled at the end of World War II, although later raised, and one of them, the *Koningen Wilhelmina,* continued to run until 1959. The twin funnelled *Oscar Huber* was withdrawn in 1966, and is now a museum at Duisburg Ruhnort, whilst *Wurtemburg* is preserved on dry land at Magdeburg.

Royal Navy paddle tugs have already been mentioned, but the Admiralty experimented with paddle warships until the screw was proved superior in 1843. Henry Bell, of *Comet* fame, had approached the Admiralty as long ago as

Now preserved at Duisburg, Oscar Huber is a typical example of a German river paddle tug — a far more elegant vessel than the squat tugs once found in British waters.

1800, but they were reluctant to accept the idea of a steamship at all. Ironically, *HMS Comet* was launched in 1822 at Deptford, as the navy's first steamship, albeit a tug. The paddle frigate *HMS Gorgon* was launched in 1837. The 1,100 ton vessel was armed with two 10 inch and four 30 pounder guns. In the present century paddle steamers have been requisitioned in each of the two world wars for service as minesweepers, troopships and even hospital ships. Impressed steamers were not confined to British coastal waters. *Walton Belle* and *London Belle* were sent to the White Sea as hospital ships in the first world war, and others patrolled in the Mediterranean. The navy was in fact so pleased with the performance of some of the pleasure steamers as minesweepers in the first world war, that they ordered a whole class of 32 purpose built ships. Known as the Racecourse class some were later adapted for use as passenger ships, for example, the *Lorna Doone* of the Red Funnel fleet, which had originally been commissioned as *HMS Atherstone*. Probably the most well known role played by many pleasure steamers and ferries was during the Dunkirk evacuation of 1940. Five excursion paddlers were lost in the event, including *Gracie Fields*, but other ships made several crossings, returning each time from the French coast laden with troops. Two of these steamers survive today, the *Medway Queen* which rescued some 7,000 men, and PS *Ryde*, built for the Southern Railway in 1937.

Yet other roles for paddle steamers have included survey ships and the more glamorous duty of Royal Yacht.

In the former category the *Triton* was launched in 1882 for the Royal Navy. She was later converted into a training ship moored at Gravesend, and was not finally scrapped until as late as 1962. Two Royal Yachts bore the name *Osborne*, and the second, a 250 feet long twin funnelled vessel of 1,850 tons built in 1874, conveyed the body of Queen Victoria from her home at Osborne across the Solent in 1901. She was replaced by a screw steamer in 1906. The first *Osborne* had originally been launched as the *Victoria and Albert*, but the name was changed in 1855.

The *Kassed Kheir* was a paddle schooner built by Thornycroft for the Egyptian Royal Family in 1926. A paddler was chosen because of the shallow River Nile.

The compound diagonal engines of Medway Queen. Like many other paddle steamers, the engine room was open to view, and the motion of the polished machinery held an almost hypnotic effect on many passengers.

PADDLE PROPULSION

The simplest form of engine employed in paddle steamers was the oscillating type, a principle often used in toy steam engines. The piston rod was connected directly to the paddle crankshaft, and the cylinder actually pivoted on a trunnion. This type of engine was quite compact, but was discarded because of limitations on the efficiency of steam tight cylinder ports as boiler pressures increased. A set of oscillating engines from PS *Empress* is preserved in Southampton Maritime Museum.

However, the oscillating engine was not the power unit used in the first steamers. Single cylinder side lever engines were sometimes installed, which were really a variation of the beam engine, but with the beam or more usually, two beams, at the side of the engine, rather than above, in order to minimise the overall height of the unit, thus keeping the centre of gravity as low as possible. Fulton had originally adapted the side lever engine idea for the *Clermont,* and Henry Bell modified the principle slightly for his *Comet* by placing the cylinder above the crankshaft. This engine is now preserved in the Science Museum.

Also preserved in the Science Museum is a two cylinder steamboat engine built by William Symington in 1788. As previously described, Symington designed and built the *Charlotte Dundas,* but he had experimented some years earlier with a steam powered vessel on Dalswinton Loch. This craft was twin hulled (one containing the engine and the other housing the boiler), with two paddle wheels in between.

In North America, the beam engine was often used for the big river steamers, and the beam itself could often be seen exposed and protruding above the super-

The oscillating engines from PS Empress were fortunately preserved at Southampton Maritime Museum when the ship was scrapped.

structure of the ship. In this role they were commonly known as 'Walking Beam Engines'.

A. & J. Inglis built two paddlers for the China Navigation Company in 1873, for use on the Yangtse river services. Named *Pekin* and *Ichang* they both had walking beam engines, with massive American style paddle boxes.

The steeple engine was also used in the 19th century. Here, the cylinder was placed vertically immediately below the crankshaft. However, the crosshead to which the piston rods were coupled was

Ichang was built for the China Navigation Co. in 1874 by the Scottish builders A&J Inglis. Apart from the massive side wheels, note the walking beam engine.

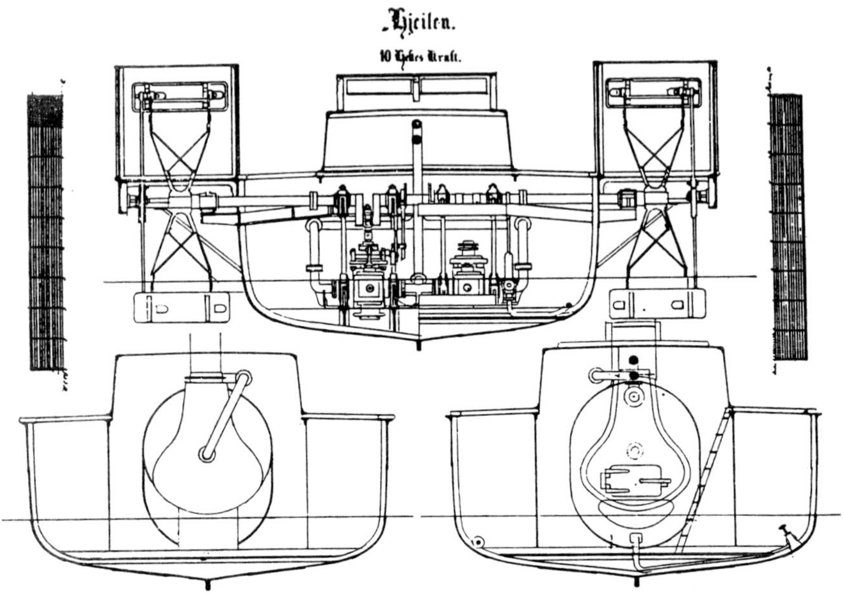

The Danish veteran Hjejlen is still powered by her original 1861 oscillating engine, although the vessel has been reboilered twice during her long life. Each cylinder has a bore of 10 inches and a 16 inch stroke, and is connected directly to the crankshaft thus resulting in the oscillating motion.

above the crankshaft, which was driven by a connecting rod from the crosshead. The engine was so named because of its vertical arrangement, and projecting piston rods.

The form of engine which later became standard was the diagonal, in which, as its name suggests, the cylinder may be positioned between the horizontal and the vertical, at a lower level than the crankshaft, which was driven by a connecting rod from the piston rod. As steam pressures increased, the idea of using the steam a second time, the principle of the compound engine, developed. Rather than use the steam in one

Although outwardly a conventional paddle steamer, Talisman was actually built in 1935 with diesel electric propulsion. A number of surviving Swiss lake paddlers have been converted from steam machinery to diesel electric over the years.

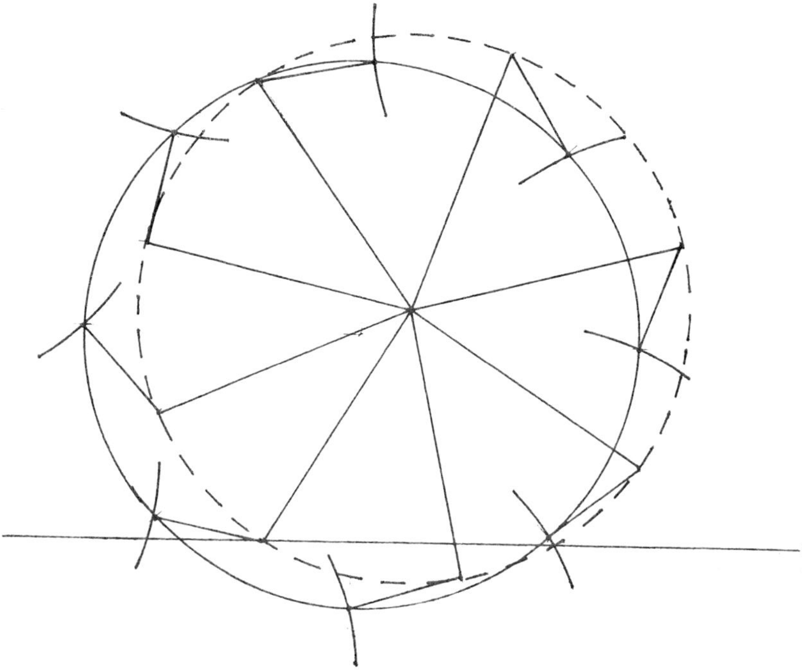

In order to increase the effort produced by the paddle floats, a feathering mechanism was designed to increase the length of time and area of each float exposed to the water during a single revolution. This was achieved by pivoting each float on the main wheel rim, and connecting them by rods to an eccentric point near the crankshaft.

cylinder and then condense it, engines were built with a second, larger, cylinder to make the steam do work for a second time, albeit at a lower pressure. One complaint often associated with the compound diagonal was a surging effect of the vessel which was overcome by the triple expansion engine, a further development of the compound, in which the steam was used for a third time, in an even larger diameter and lower pressure cylinder.

In 1935 *Talisman* was ordered by the London & North Eastern Railway. Outwardly with the appearance of a conventional paddle steamer, she was in fact diesel electric, and proved to be an economical ship to run. Other diesel electric paddlers were the Royal Navy tugs built in the 1950s, whilst in Switzerland *Genève* on Lake Geneva was coverted from steam to diesel electric propulsion in 1934, and several other vessels have subsequently been so modified.

Mention should also be made of the principle of feathering paddle wheels. In order to improve the efficiency of the wheel, each float is pivoted about the rim and connected by a rod to an eccentric on the paddle shaft. This means that the float maintains a more vertical position during contact with the water, thus presenting a greater surface area for a longer period of time. Designers and builders in the USA, however, persisted in large diameter fixed float wheels long after the general acceptance of feathering.

A detail of one of PS Ryde's paddle wheels, showing the feathering mechanism. Although many later paddlers used steel floats, others (including Waverley) still used wood floats.

KD's last paddle steamer Goethe is seen here in typical Rhineland setting. She was sunk by a bomb attack in 1945, but was rebuilt, lengthened and re-entered service in 1952. She continued to operate regularly from Cologne to Koblenz until laid up in 1989.

DECLINE

The story of the paddle steamer since the second world war has essentially been one of decline.

Many vessels impressed for naval service were returned to civilian duties, but others had been lost or were beyond economic repair. Several orders were placed for new ships, for example the *Bristol Queen* and *Cardiff Queen* mentioned earlier, and the *Waverley* for the LNER. *Waverley* was based on an earlier design, and in many respects could be regarded as obsolete before she was built. The paddle boxes of the two new Campbell ships were disguised with dummy portholes, rather than the traditional styling, as if to hide the fact that they were indeed paddlers.

The last passenger paddle steamer built in the UK was *Maid of the Loch* for Loch Lomond in 1954, which unusually had a lightweight aluminium superstructure.

However, holiday patterns were changing the demand for excursion steamers which were becoming uneconomic to run, and by the late 1960s only a handful of paddlers remained in operation. The south coast's last one, PS *Ryde*, carried her final passengers at the end of the 1969 season, but a brave attempt to revive Thames sailings was made in 1965 with *Jeanie Deans*, built for the Clyde in 1931, and renamed *Queen of the South*. The venture only lasted for one season before the ship was sold for scrap.

At the end of 1973, *Waverley* was withdrawn from service, but fortunately passed into the care of the Paddle Steamer Preservation Society, who since 1975 have operated her each season, not only in her native Scotland, but around many other parts of the British coastline. The former River Dart steamer *Kingswear Castle* has also been preserved by the society and this delightful little ship is based on the Medway. Early attempts to preserve the *Medway Queen* resulted in the ship becoming a nightclub at a marina on the Isle of Wight. However, the ship was replaced in that role by the *Ryde*, and by the early 1980s she lay derelict. A second rescue bid was made, and the ship was refloated, placed on a pontoon, and taken back to the River Medway for eventual restoration.

In 1962 a full size replica of *Comet* was constructed to celebrate the 150th anniversary of the original ship, and although steamed for a time she is now kept on dry land at Port Glasgow. More recently, another replica has been built in Australia as part of the bicentennial celebrations. It is named *William the*

Schonnbrun dates from 1911, and is the last survivor of the DDSG's once large fleet of paddle steamers operating on the Danube.

Fourth, and the original vessel was launched in 1831. Other ships have survived in the UK in static roles. *Tattershall Castle*, *Caledonia* and *Princess Elizabeth* all retired to the Thames as floating restaurants, although *Caledonia* was destroyed by fire in 1980, and *Princess Elizabeth* now has a new home in France.

Whilst there are so few active steamers in UK waters, a surprising number of lake and river paddle steamers are still operating, or are actively preserved on the continent.

Dating from 1856, *Skibladner* still operates on Lake Mjosa in Norway. The 165 feet long vessel has triple expansion engines fitted in 1888, when she lost one of her two original funnels. Five years her junior is *Hjejlen,* a diminutive steamer of only 39 tons, and in remarkably original condition, which sails on

Dresden pictured waiting to depart from the port from which she takes her name. She was built in 1926, and has a capacity for up to 1,300 passengers.

Another of the Weisse Flotte ships operating on the Elbe is Meissen, clearly demonstrating how funnels and masts are lowered to negotiate bridges!

the Silkeborg Lakes in Denmark. She is coal fired, and has a two cylinder oscillating engine.

Switzerland can offer paddle steamer services on five lakes. The 1848 built *Rigi* is displayed at the Swiss Transport Museum, where the engines and boiler of another ship, *Pilatus*, are also on show. Some of the Swiss ships have been converted from steam to diesel propulsion, but others are in very original order, and one or two of the diesel ships have now had their original tall funnels restored, to give an outwardly more authentic appearance.

Lake Geneva not only caters for tourist

Not the most elegant of ships perhaps, Avoca was originally built in 1877 to carry grain on the Murray River. With an appearance now much altered, and styled Showboat Avoca, she is regularly used for cruises and special functions.

Murray River Cruises operate the 1700 ton Murray Princess. The Mississippi style stern wheeler offers a programme of six day cruises from Renmart, South Australia.

traffic, but many workers commute across the lake each day, and paddlers are still often rostered for these morning and evening duties, with day cruises in between. Flagship of the fleet here is *La Suisse,* built in 1910, whilst *Simplon,* ten years younger is the largest of all the Swiss steamers, with a capacity of 1,500 passengers.

Lake Brienz has only one paddle steamer, the *Lotschberg,* built in 1914, but five ships are still in operation on Lake Lucerne, and like all the other Swiss ships are immaculately maintained. All have full restaurant facilities, and they are two class ships. *Unterwalden* of 1902 is probably the finest of all, although she came perilously close to being with-

Skibladner is a delightful veteran built for operation on Norway's Lake Mjosa in 1856. She was re-engined in 1888 when one of her two original funnels was removed.

Sailing regularly from Silkeborg in Denmark, is Hjejlen, also built in 1856. A mere 39 tons gross, she is still coal fired, and fitted with oscillating engines.

drawn in 1977, when a new motorship actually took her name.

The Lucerne ships, and indeed some other river steamers, have telescopic or folding funnels and masts, to allow them to pass under low bridges. Lake Zurich is the home of *Stadt Zurich* and *Stadt Rapperswil,* dating from 1909 and 1914 respectively.

Another 19th century vessel, *Gisela,* has returned to service in Austria. She was not withdrawn until 1980, but her future at that time looked very uncertain. She was built in 1871, is still coal fired, and has oscillating engines. PS *Hohentwiel* has recently been restored at Hard, Lake Constance, whilst another veteran, albeit now diesel electric, is the *Kaiser Franz Josef 1* on Wolfgangsee. The last Austrian paddle steamer on the Danube is *Schonbrun,* built at Budapest in 1911.

Piedmonte still sees occasional service on Lake Maggiore in Italy. She was built at Zurich by Escher Wyss in 1904, and was originally named Regina Madre.

Built at Dresden in 1900 for service on the River Weser, Kaiser Wilhelm has been restored at Lauenberg. Her preservation society owners use her regularly during the summer months, and the ship is pictured here near Bleckede.

On the Rhine, *Goethe* was the last paddle steamer in operation, although she was laid up for the 1990 season, and did not take up her usual duties between Cologne and Koblenz. She has a capacity of 1,600 passengers, and was lengthened during a rebuild following sinking in a bombing raid in 1945. *Kaiser Wilhelm*, a veteran of 1900, and still coal fired, is preserved in operational order at Lauenberg, on the River Elbe.

Piemonte is a pretty little steamer dating from 1904, and based at Lake Maggiore in Italy, which only sees very occasional use. However, *Patria* and *Concordia* are used much more regularly

Gisela was extensively restored by a group of steamer enthusiasts returning to steam on Austria's Traunsee in 1986. She was originally built in 1871 by an Englishman, Joseph Ruston.

on Lake Como, whilst Lake Garda has two diesel electric paddle ships, plus another former paddle steamer which now features screw propulsion.

Turning now to the former East Germany, a fascinating fleet of veteran steamers survive in the Weisse Flotte (White Fleet), on the River Elbe at Dresden. Many date from the 19th century, with oscillating engines, and are coal fired. The longest trip operated is a two-day run to Urstig in Czechoslovakia. Like some of the Lake Lucerne steamers, the ships have to be able to pass under some low bridges, and therefore they have collapsible masts and funnels. Oldest of the fleet is *Stadt Wehlen,* dating from 1879.

The president of North Korea visited East Germany in 1984, and subsequently ordered a replica of PS *Dresden.* Named *Phongjang* it was completed two years later.

Four paddle steamers were based on the Vltava in Czechoslovakia, the *Devin, Vysehard, Vltava* and *Labe,* all dating from the period 1938-49. Not the most elegant of ships, *Labe,* the last to be coal fired, was withdrawn in 1987, *Vysehard* following a year later, and in 1989 *Vltava* suffered a boiler explosion.

An interesting vessel in Bulgaria is *Radetsky,* originally a paddle tug, but rebuilt as a replica of the ship of that name of 1851. The original *Radetsky* had been hijacked in 1876 by Bulgarian Freedom Fighters in the campaign to gain Bulgarian independence.

Quite a number of other paddle steamers survive as restaurant ships, or even as yacht club headquarters, sometimes drastically altered and losing their character. Some examples of those better preserved are *Plinio* at Calico, on Lake Como, *Johann Strauss* in Vienna, and *Wilhelm Tell* at Lucerne.

FURTHER READING

Condie, Allan T. *Paddle Steamers in Camera.* Allan T. Condie Publications, 1989.
Coombes, Nigel. *Passenger Steamers of the Bristol Channel.* Twelveheads Press, 1990.
Cox, Bernard. *Paddle Steamers.* Blandford Press, 1979.
Cox, Bernard. *Pleasure Steamers.*
Deayton, Alistair. *Steamships of Europe.* Conway Maritime Press, 1988.
Dumpleton, Bernard. *The Story of the Paddle Steamer.* Colin Venton, 1973.
Guthrie, John. *Bizarre Ships of the Nineteenth Century.* Hutchinson, 1970.
Paterson, Alan J. S. *The Golden Years of the Clyde Steamers.* David & Charles, 1969.
Paterson, Alan J. S. *Victorian Summer of the Clyde Steamers.* David & Charles, 1972.
Ransom, P. J. G. *The Archaeology of the Transport Revolution 1750-1850.* Guild Publishing, 1984.

MAGAZINES

PADDLE WHEELS is the quarterly journal of the Paddle Steamer Preservation Society.

SOCIETIES

Paddle Steamer Preservation Society Membership Secretary: Rev. C. Robb, The Manse, Sorn Road, Catrine, Mauchline, Ayrshire KA5 6NA.
Medway Queen Preservation Society, 88 Bicknor Road, Maidstone, Kent.

PLACES TO VISIT

MUSEUMS

Blackgang Sawmill & St. Catherine's Quay, Blackgang, Isle of Wight. Tel. (0983) 730330. Reconstructed engine room of PS *Compton Castle.*

Chatham Historic Dockyard, Chatham, Kent. Tel. (0634) 812551. Home of PS *Kingswear Castle* (see separate entry) and PT *John H. Amos.*

Glasgow Museum of Transport, Kelvin Hall, Bunhouse Road, Glasgow. Tel. (041-357) 3929. Side lever engine from PS *Industry.*

Hollycombe Steam Collection, Midhurst Road, Liphook, Hants. Tel. (04203) 4740 and (0428) 724900. Engines from PS *Caledonia.*

National Maritime Museum, Romney Road, London SE10 9NF. tel. (081-858) 4422. Paddle tug *Reliant.*

Science Museum, Exhibition Road, South Kensington, London SW7 2DD. Tel. (071-938) 8000. Engines from PS *Comet* and 1788 engine by William Symington.

Southampton Maritime Museum, Town Quay, Southampton. Engines from PS *Empress.*

SHIPS

PS *Kingswear Castle* operates excursions in the Thames and Medway areas. Details from Kingswear Castle Excursions Ltd., Chatham Historic Dockyard, Chatham, Kent. Tel. (0634) 827648.

PS *Waverley* operates excursions around many parts of the UK coast. Timetable information from Waverley Excursions Ltd., Waverley Terminal, Anderstons Quay, Glasgow. Tel. (041-221) 8152.

PS *Tattershall Castle,* Victoria Embankment, London SW1A 2HR. Preserved steamer moored as conference and function venue.

PS *Medway Queen* undergoing restoration on River Medway. Visits by prior arrangement with Medway Queen Preservation Society.

PS *Wingfield Castle,* Jackson Dock Hartlepool, statically preserved steamer. Tourist Information Office. Tel. (0429) 266522.

STEAMER HOLIDAYS

Vintage Tours, 79 Great Preston Road, Ryde, Isle of Wight PO33 1EF. Tel. (0983) 65082. Itineraries include tours of Switzerland featuring the lake paddle steamers.